Digestive System

by Grace Hansen

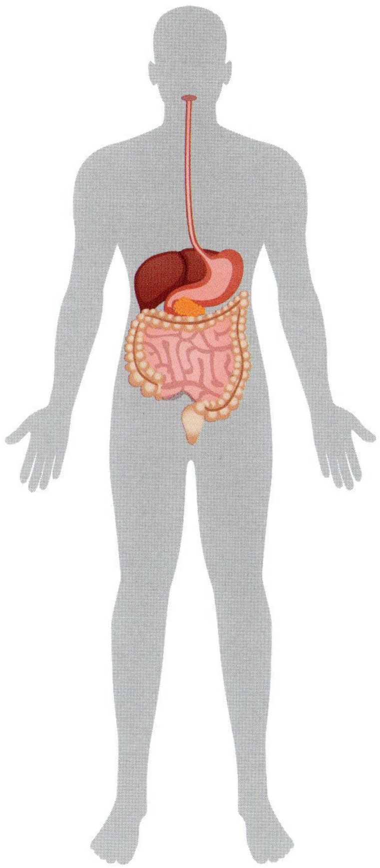

Abdo Kids
BEGINNING SCIENCE: BODY SYSTEMS

Abdo Kids Jumbo is an Imprint of Abdo Kids
abdobooks.com

abdobooks.com

Published by Abdo Kids, a division of ABDO, P.O. Box 398166, Minneapolis, Minnesota 55439.

102018

012019

THIS BOOK CONTAINS RECYCLED MATERIALS

Photo Credits: Alamy, iStock, Science Source, Shutterstock

Production Contributors: Teddy Borth, Jennie Forsberg, Grace Hansen

Design Contributors: Dorothy Toth, Laura Mitchell

Library of Congress Control Number: 2018945948

Publisher's Cataloging-in-Publication Data

Names: Hansen, Grace, author.

Title: Digestive system / by Grace Hansen.

Description: Minneapolis, Minnesota : Abdo Kids, 2019 | Series: Beginning science: body systems | Includes glossary, index and online resources (page 24).

Identifiers: ISBN 9781532181856 (lib. bdg.) | ISBN 9781532182839 (ebook) | ISBN 9781532183324 (Read-to-me ebook)

Subjects: LCSH: Digestive organs--Juvenile literature. | Digestive system--Juvenile literature. | Digestion--Juvenile literature. | Gastrointestinal system--Juvenile literature.

Classification: DDC 612.3--dc23

Table of Contents

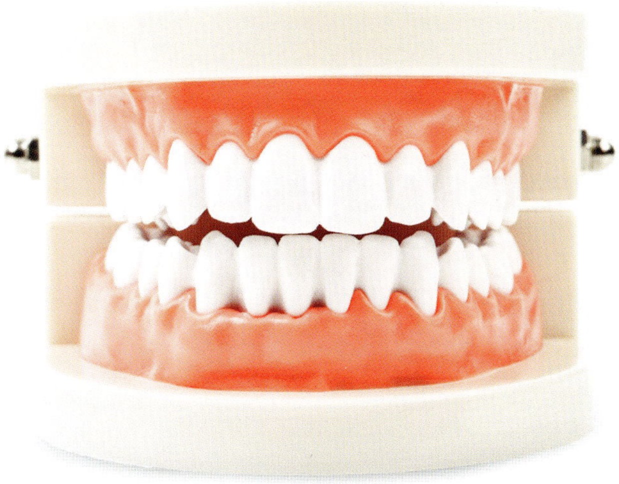

The Digestive System

The digestive system changes food into fuel for your body. It makes sure your body gets the **nutrients** it needs from the food you eat.

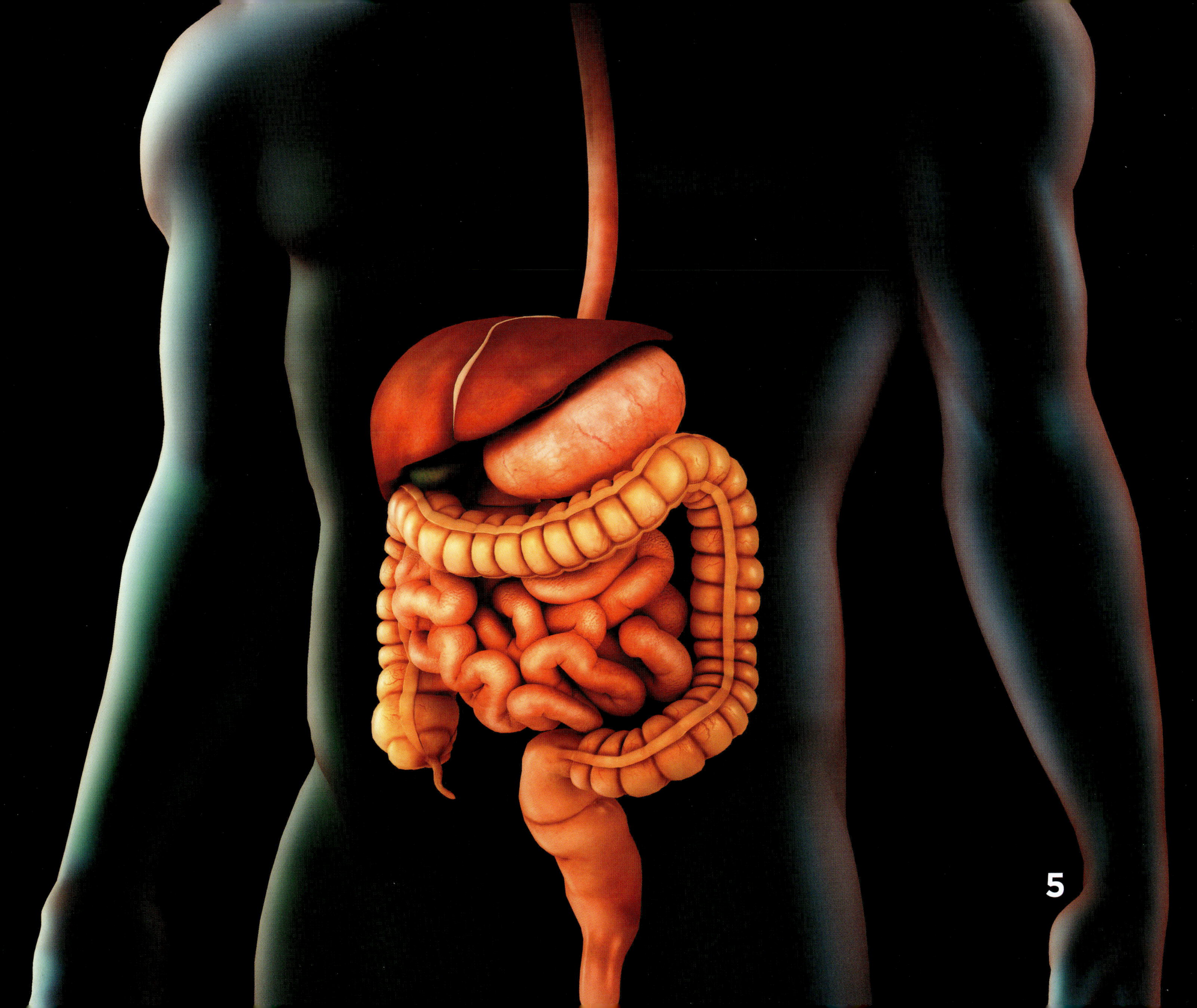

Digestion begins before you take your first bite. Your mouth creates saliva to help swallow your food. Your brain tells your stomach to start producing **acid**.

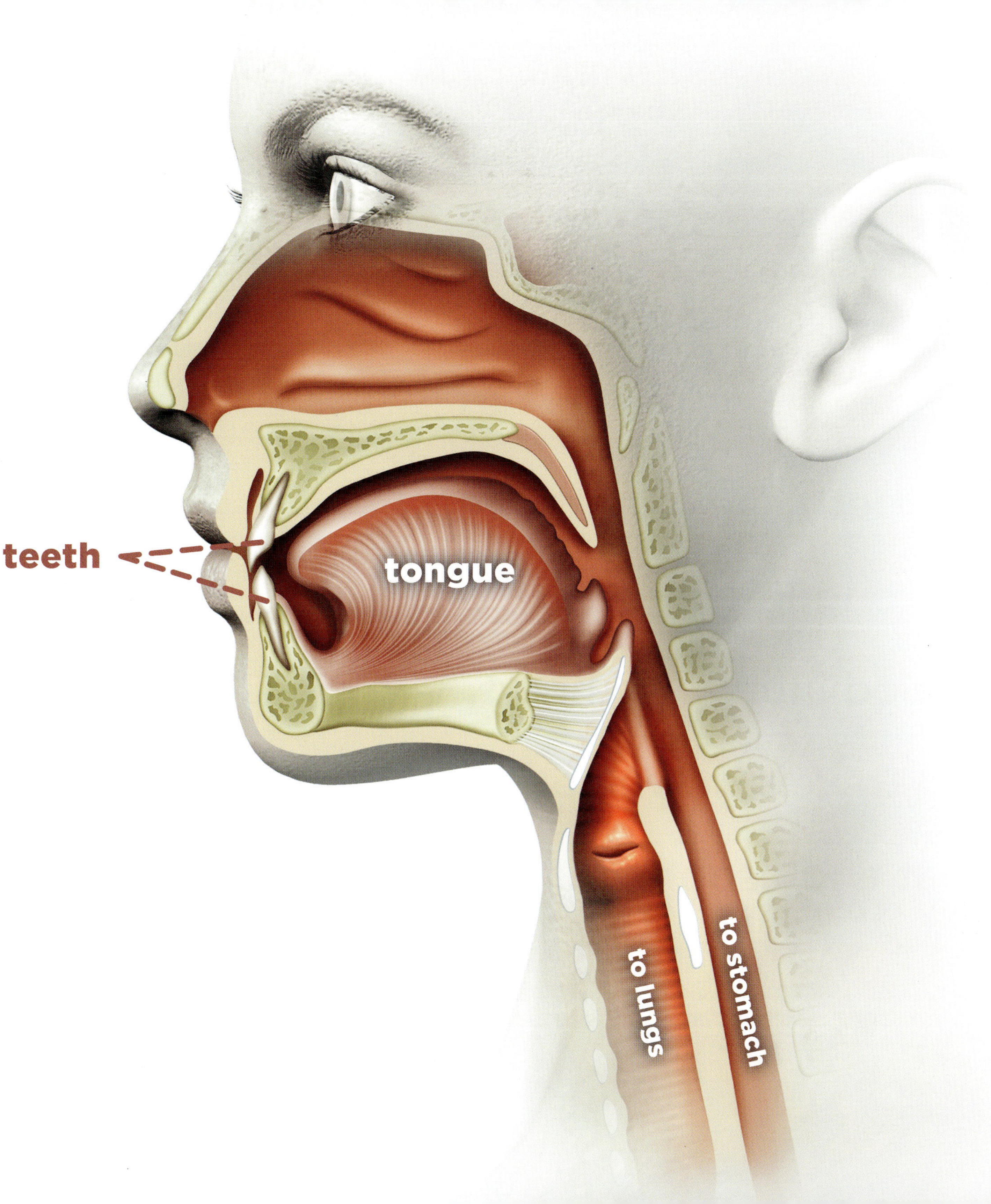
teeth
tongue
to lungs
to stomach

Chew Well!

Your teeth chew up the food. Your tongue and mouth push the food into your throat. Food travels down your throat and esophagus.

The Stomach & Intestines

Food then enters your stomach. Muscles mix the food with **gastric acids** and **enzymes**. These break the food down.

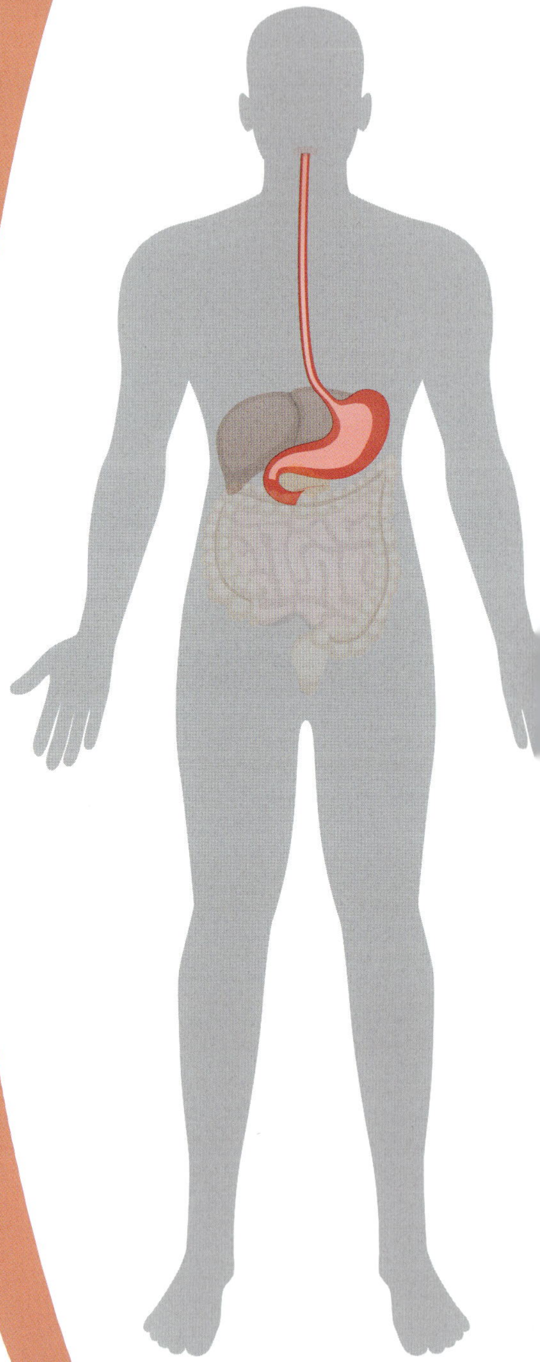

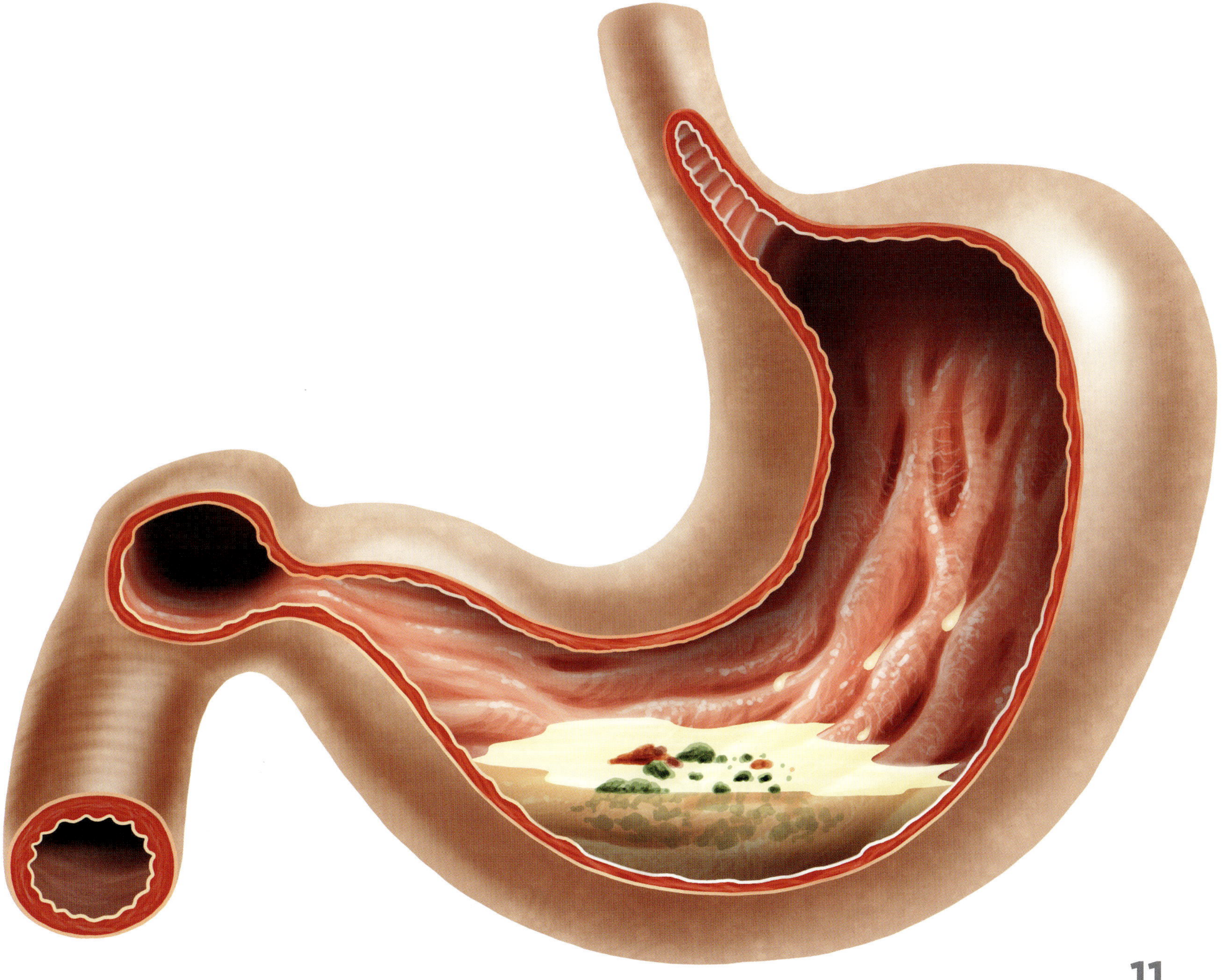

The food is now called chyme. It leaves your stomach through the **pylorus**. It moves into the small intestine.

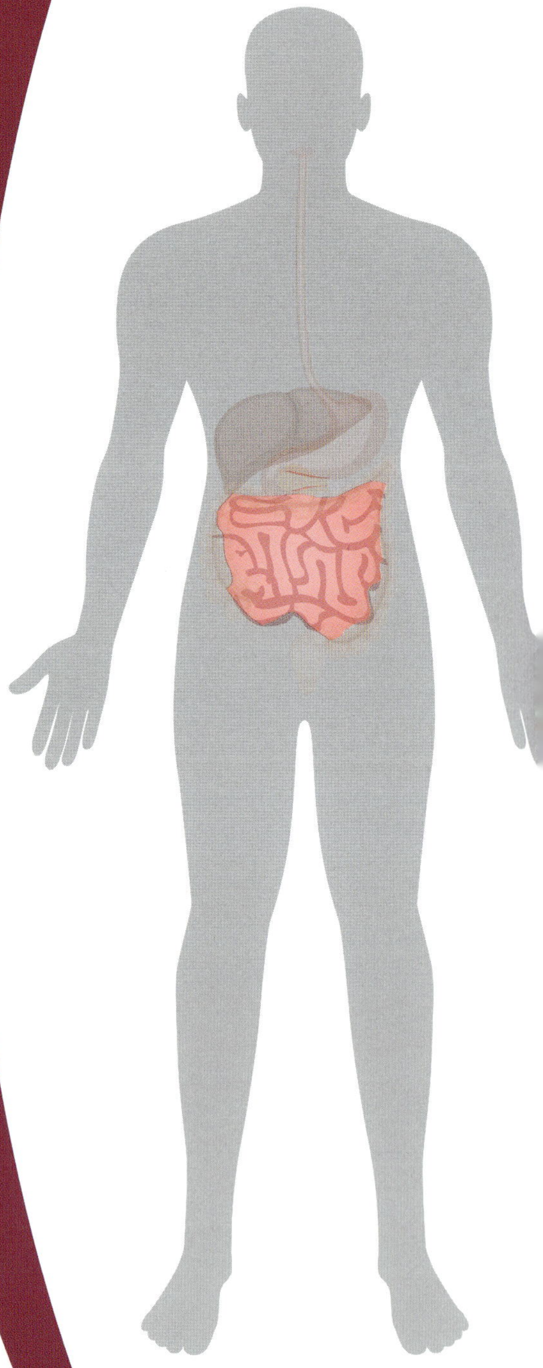

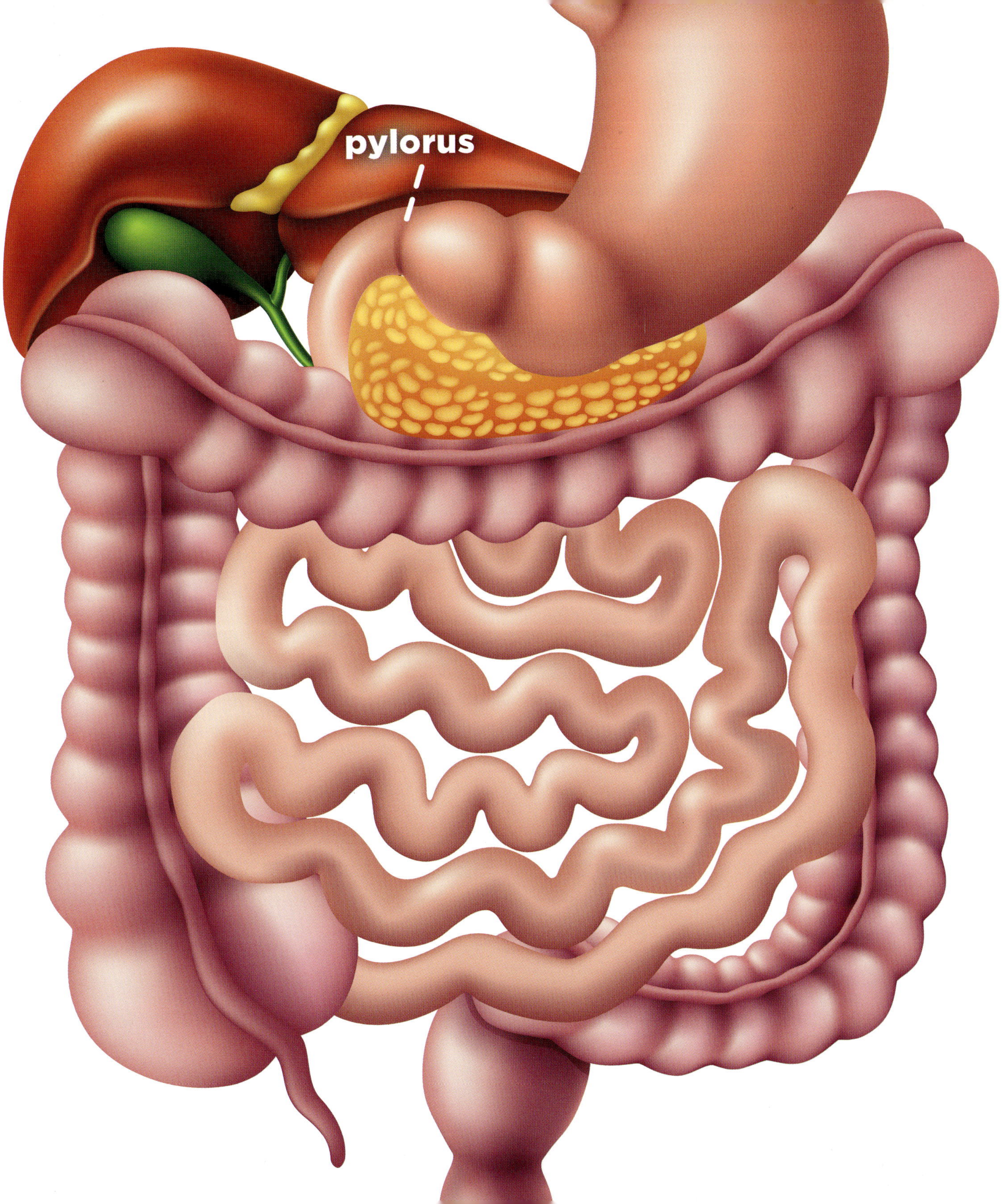
pylorus

The small intestine is lined with villi. These tiny bulges take in **nutrients**. The nutrients enter your bloodstream. The blood carries them throughout your body.

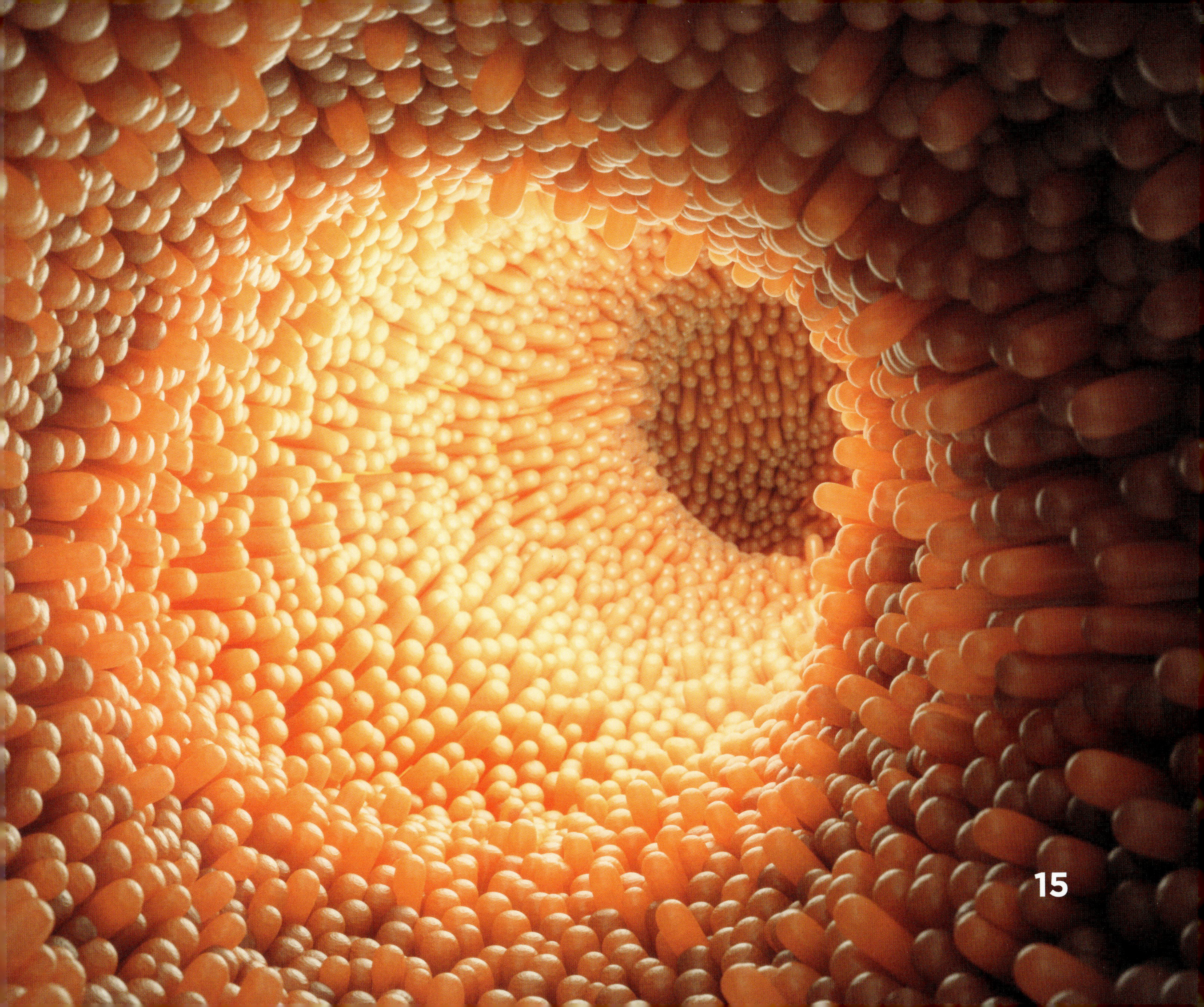

The remaining matter moves to the large intestine. Your large intestine stores lots of good **bacteria**. The bacteria can break down the food even more. This process can create gas!

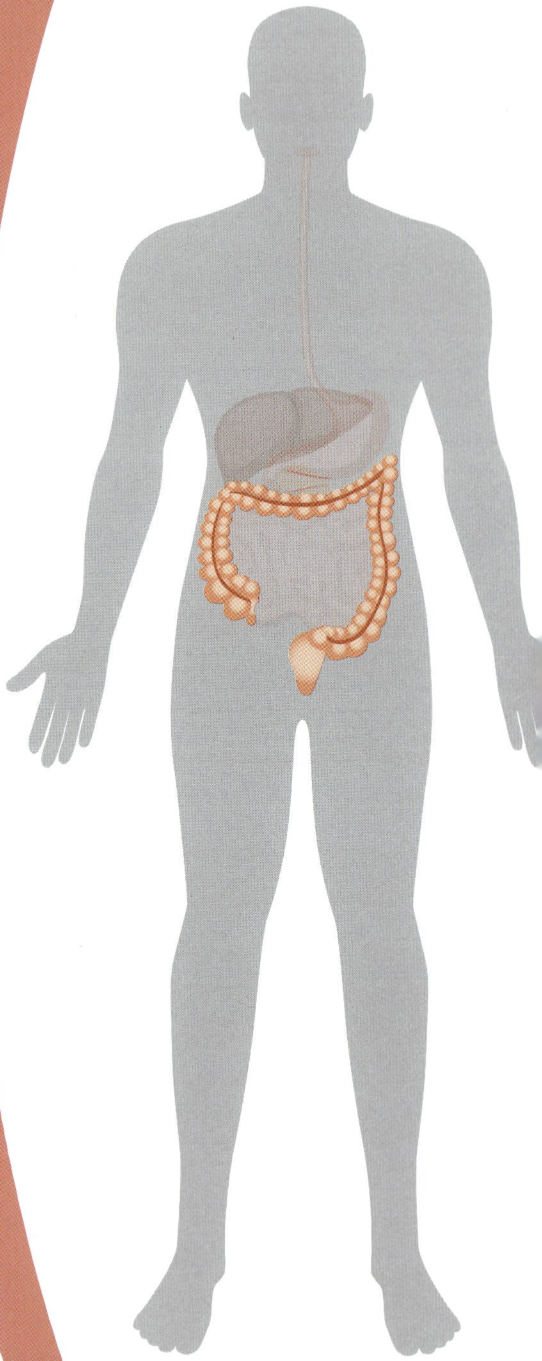

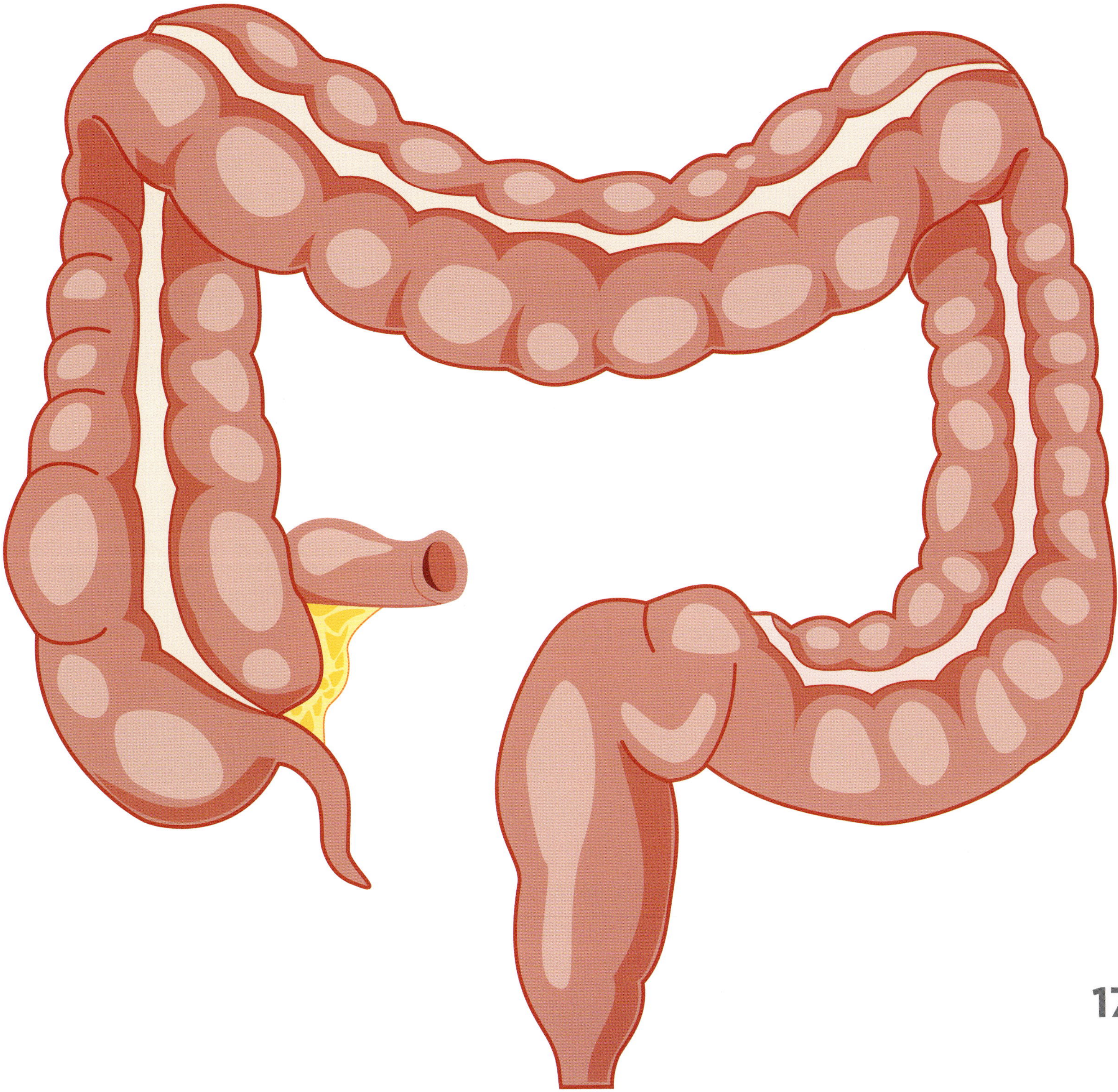

Microvilli in the large intestine help remove water from the matter. This creates solid waste.

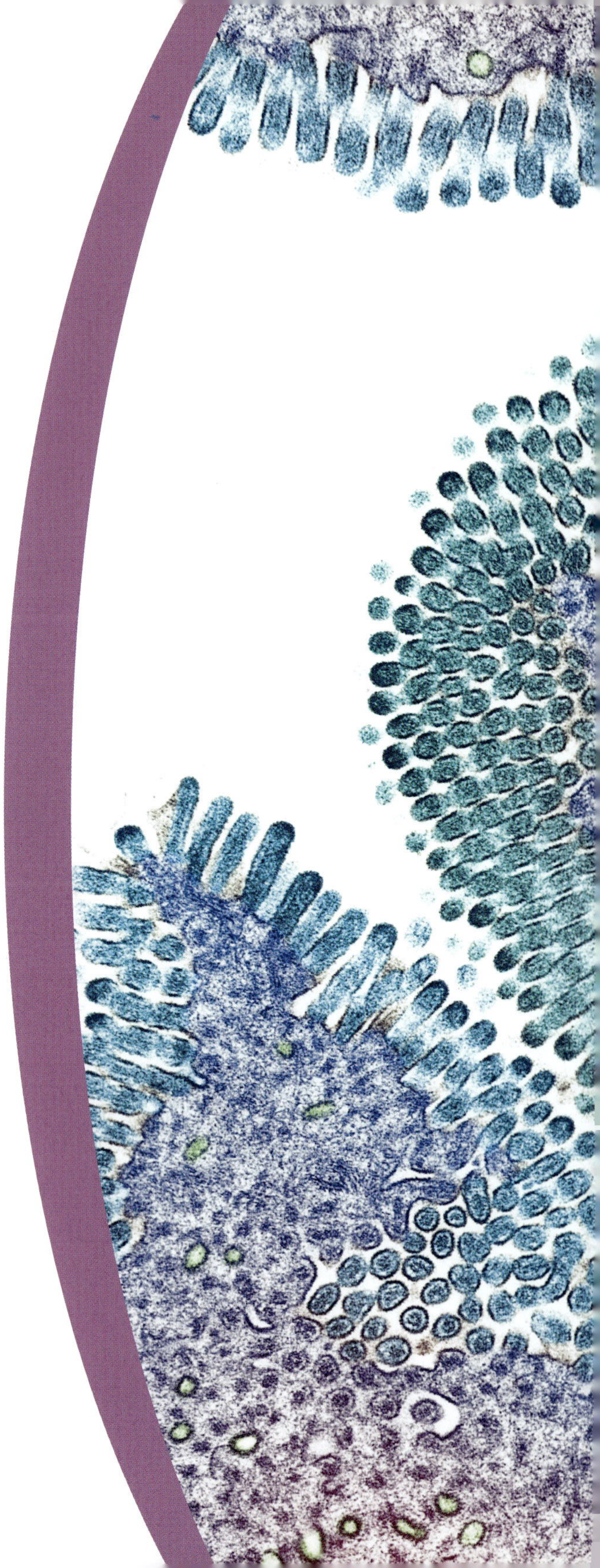

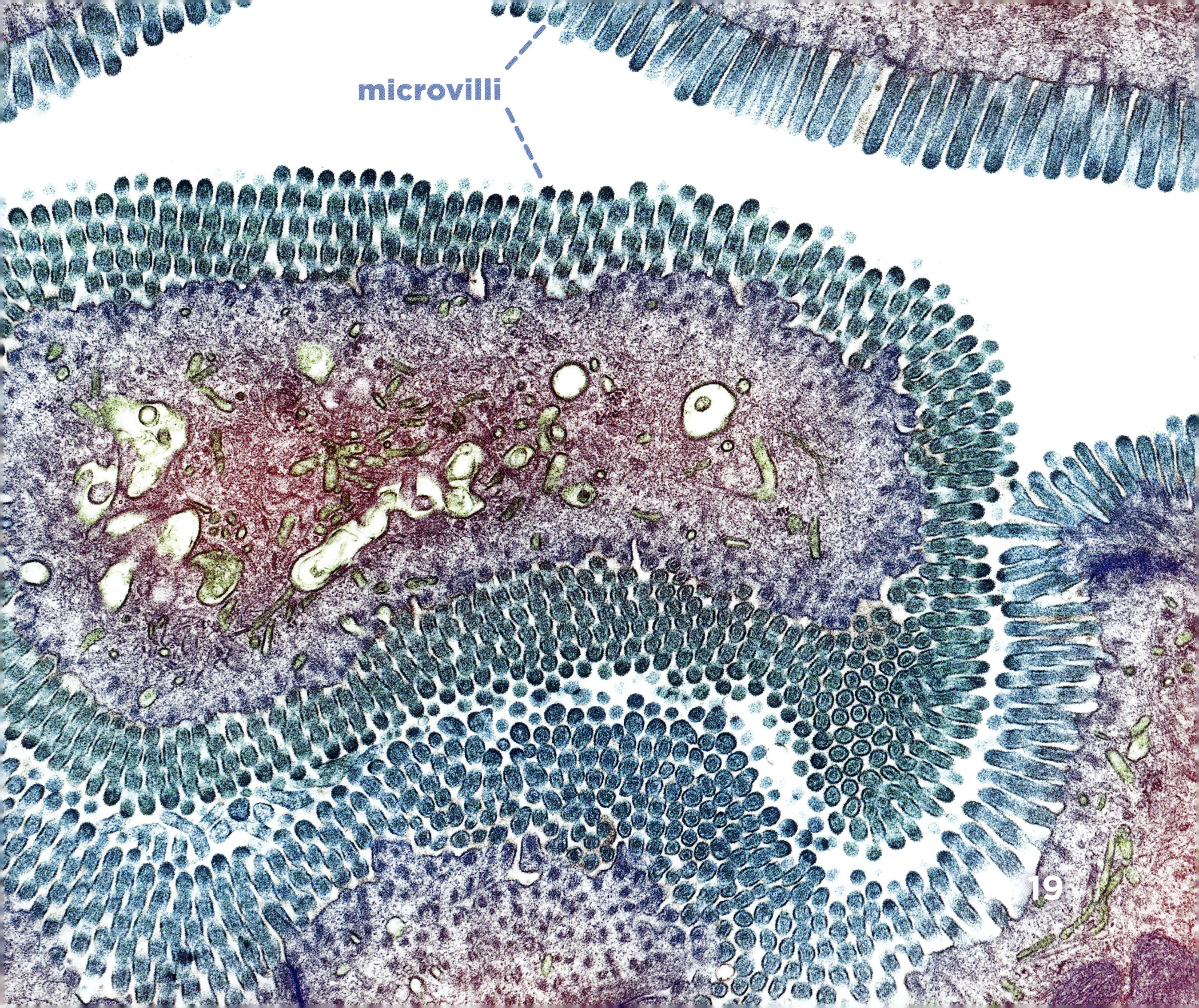
microvilli

The large intestine has one final job. It sends solid waste out of your body.

Let's Review!

- The digestive system takes the food you eat and breaks it down into **nutrients** that your body can use.
- The nutrients in food give your body's cells the energy they need to work.
- Your teeth chew up food. Your saliva makes it wet so it is easy to swallow. Your tongue pushes the food into your throat.
- Your small intestine breaks down and absorbs the most nutrients.

Glossary

bacteria – in the intestines, a microorganism that helps digest food, absorbs nutrients, keeps bad bacteria out, and more.

enzyme – a substance that helps speed up chemical reactions in the body.

gastric acid – a digestive fluid with ingredients that help destroy bacteria and break down the proteins in food.

nutrient – a substance that gives nourishment essential for growth and the upkeep of life.

pylorus – the opening from the stomach into the small intestine.

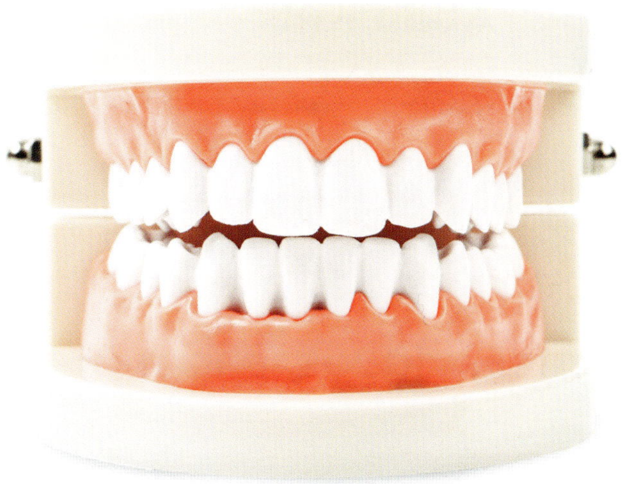

Index